WE READ ABOUT

BEES

Kim Thompson and Madison Parker

TABLE OF CONTENTS

SEAHORSE
PUBLISHING

Parent and Caregiver Guide

Reading aloud with your child has many benefits. It expands vocabulary, sparks discussion, and promotes an emotional bond. Research shows that children who have books read aloud to them have improved language skills, leading to greater school success.

I Read! You Read! books offer a fun and easy way to read with your child. Follow these guidelines.

Before Reading

- Look at the front and back covers. Discuss personal experiences that relate to the topic.
- Read the *Words to Know* on page 3. Talk about what the words mean.
- If the book will be challenging or unfamiliar to your child, read it aloud by yourself the first time. Then, invite your child to participate in a second reading.

During Reading

CHILD Have your child read the words beside this symbol. This text has been carefully matched to the reading and grade levels shown on the cover.

ADULT You read the words beside this symbol.

- Stop often to discuss what you are reading and to make sure your child understands.
- If your child struggles with decoding a word, help them sound it out. If it is still a challenge, say the word for your child and have them repeat it after you.
- To find the meaning of a word, look for clues in the surrounding words and pictures.

After Reading

- Praise your child's efforts. Notice how they have grown as a reader.
- Ask and answer questions about the book.
- Discuss what your child learned and what they liked or didn't like about the book.

Most importantly, let your child know that reading is fun and worthwhile. Keep reading together as your child's skills and confidence grow.

WORDS TO KNOW

 bee

 beehive

 flower

 honey

 wings

SIGHT WORDS

a	find	have	make
away	fly	in	what
can	go	little	you

What can you find in a **flower**?

A **flower** is where a plant has its seeds.

flower

You can find a little **bee**! CHILD

Bees are insects. Insects have six legs. ADULT

bee

Bees have **wings**. CHILD

A bee has four **wings** that help it fly from flower to flower. ADULT

wing

Bees go in a **beehive**. CHILD

Bees work and sleep in the **beehive**. ADULT

beehive

Bees make **honey**. CHILD

Sweet **honey** is made from the nectar of flowers. ADULT

honey

A bee can fly away!

CHILD

Bees fly as fast as 20 miles (32 kilometers) per hour!

ADULT

Index

Written by: Kim Thompson and Madison Parker
Design by: Under the Oaks Media
Series Development: James Earley

Photos: herain Kanthatham: cover; Anton Nikitinskiy: p. 5; Jack Hong: p. 7; Mircea Costina: p. 9; nicemyphoto: p. 11; STARsoft: p. 13; ETgohome: p. 15

Library of Congress PCN Data
We Read About Bees / Kim Thompson and Madison Parker
I Read! You Read!
ISBN 979-8-8873-5184-1(hard cover)
ISBN 979-8-8873-5204-6(paperback)
ISBN 979-8-8873-5224-4(EPUB)
ISBN 979-8-8873-5244-2(eBook)
Library of Congress Control Number: 2022945539
Printed in China

Seahorse Publishing Company

www.seahorsepub.com   1-800-387-7650

Published in the United States
Seahorse Publishing
PO Box 771325
Coral Springs, FL 33077

SEAHORSE PUBLISHING